# Goats

by Robin Nelson

first step nonfiction

Lerner Publications Company · Minneapolis

What lives on a farm?

Goats live on a farm.

A female goat is a **doe**.

A male goat is a **buck**.

A doe has an **udder**.

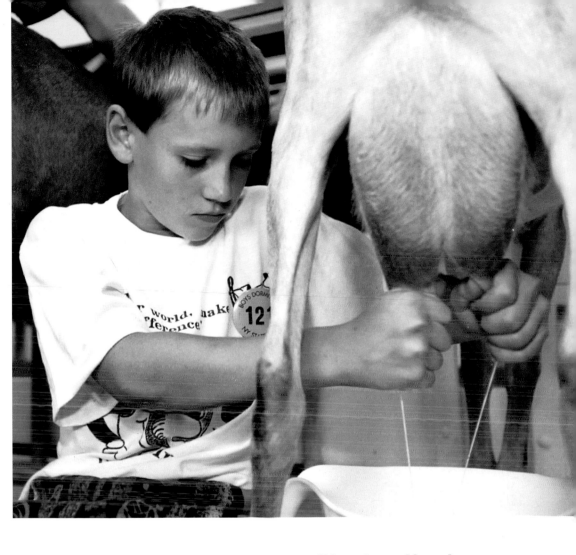

Does have milk in their
udders.

Some goats have horns.

A goat's foot is called
a **hoof**.

Goats eat grass and hay.

Goats drink a lot of water.

A baby goat drinks its
mother's milk.

A baby goat is called
a **kid**.

Farmers milk the goats.

Sometimes machines milk the goats.

Goats give us milk to drink.

It is fun to see goats on the farm!

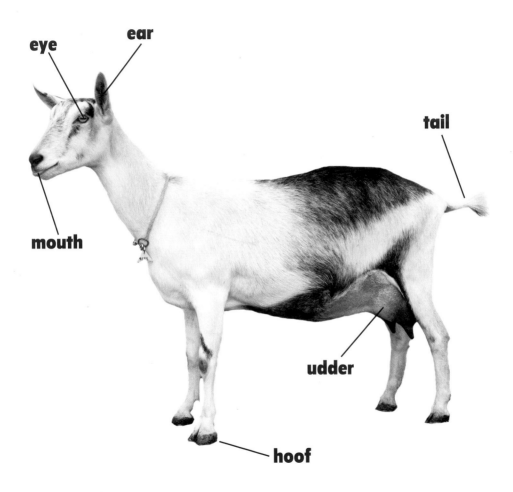

eye

ear

tail

mouth

udder

hoof

# Parts of a Goat

There are many different kinds of goats. Goats can be many different colors—brown, black, gray, red, and white. Some goats have short ears, and some have long ears. Goats have horns, but some farmers remove them so goats won't hurt one another.

# Goat Facts

 A group of goats is called a herd.

 There are more than 600 kinds of goats!

 A doe must have a kid to start making milk.

 Does are milked two times a day.

 A doe can give a gallon of milk every day.

Goats' milk is used to make cheese and even chocolate.

 Some goats are raised for their down, or hair.

 Goats are very picky eaters.

 Goats are great swimmers.

# Glossary

 **buck** – a male goat

 **doe** – a female goat

 **hoof** – a goat's foot

 **kid** – a baby goat

 **udder** – a bag of skin under a goat's belly that makes milk

# Index

The photographs in this book are reproduced through the courtesy of: © Tom Brakefeild/SuperStock, p. 2; Dave Penman/Rex Features USA, p. 3; © Karlene Schwartz, pp. 4, 5, 9, 22 (top 3 photos); © Inga Spence/Visuals Unlimited, Inc., pp. 6, 11, 15, 18, 22 (bottom); © Syracuse Newspapers/ Randi Anglin/The Image Works, p. 7; E.M. Welch/Rex Features USA, p. 8; © iStockphoto.com/ Lilli Day, p. 10; © Chucky/Dreamstime.com, p. 12; © iStockphoto.com/Ronda Tyree, pp. 13, 22 (second from bottom) ; © Verner Soler/drr.net, p. 14; © iStockphoto.com/Nina Shannon, p. 16; David W. Hamilton/Rex Features USA, p. 17.
Front cover: © Lena Ason/Alamy.

Lerner Publications Company
A division of Lerner Publishing Group, Inc.
241 First Avenue North
Minneapolis, MN 55401 U.S.A.

Website address: www.lernerbooks.com

Library of Congress Cataloging-in-Publication Data

Nelson, Robin, 1971–
    Goats / by Robin Nelson.
       p.   cm. — (First step nonfiction. Farm animals)
    Includes index.
    ISBN 978–0–7613–4061–4 (lib. bdg. : alk. paper)
    1. Goats—Juvenile literature. I. Title.
    SF383.35.N45 2009
    636.3'9—dc22                             2008024738

Manufactured in the United States of America
1 2 3 4 5 6 – DP – 14 13 12 11 10 09